THE SUNKEN PLACE

Overcoming Midlife Crisis In Marriage

SARITA SASHINGTON

Published by Victorious You Press™

Unless otherwise indicated, scripture quotations are from the Holy Bible, New King James Version. All rights reserved.

Printed in the United States of America

ISBN: _ 978-1-952756-45-0

For details email vyp.joantrandall@gmail.com
or visit us at www.victoriousyoupress.com

Dedication

To my Parents, Thomas & Shirley Brewer

And my Grandparents, Willis H. & Annie Searcy

Acknowledgments

To the Lord my God who is good and whose mercy endures forever. He is a master at refreshing and renewing anything you put in HIS hands. He who promised is faithful, and I am so grateful. He's a good, good father!

Special thanks to my little sister Monique who held me down for four years. Thank you for every prayer, for being my safe place when I needed to vent. Thank you for loving Greg and me equally, for being unbiased, and for standing in the gap for us, both individually and collectively. To Marie Marie and Underdog for being my sounding board, for warring with me for my brother in Christ and our marriage, for giving me a husband's perspective, and always using the Word to help me focus on Daddy God. For reminding me to be of good courage and to wait, I say wait on the LORD!

To my brother in Christ and husband, Greg, who worked tirelessly to reassure me of my place in his life, who goes above and beyond to make me feel safe, secure, and loved.

If I told you my story
You would hear Hope that wouldn't let go
And if I told you my story
You would hear Love that never gave up
And if I told you my story
You would hear Life, but it wasn't mine
My Story~ Big Daddy Weave

Table Of Contents

Introduction

Midlife Crisis

A period of psychological distress thought to occur in some individuals during the middle years of adulthood, roughly from ages thirty-five to sixty-five. Causes may include significant life events and health or occupational problems and concerns. American Psychological Association (APA). Some Mental health experts refer to it as a type of nervous breakdown for men.

Why am I writing this book?

One of the things I have always loved about our marriage was our ability to be transparent with our struggles. As we overcame, we helped others to overcome by sharing our story.

In twenty-two years of marriage, this was absolutely the darkest time of our marriage. We managed to survive my infidelity, a tour in Iraq during Operation Freedom, and the aftermath of that tour. And yet, none of those moments scared me like the thought of losing my marriage to some unseen entity.

For years, Greg and I sat on the front row of our section in our church and watched the marriages of our friends who have been married twenty or more years disintegrate. We would ask ourselves what happens once you hit twenty-plus years that causes such turmoil that you would throw everything you worked for down the drain. One couple comes to mind. Every Sunday, the husband would walk past our seats on the front row of our section. We noticed him dressing and acting younger. He started taking acting classes. He wore his hair and his clothes different. He seemed as if he didn't have a care in the world. Greg and I talked about the changes we had noticed. A year later, he and his wife of over twenty years were divorced; not long after that, he was remarried.

Today, I think back to that friend; that couple. I think about Greg and me and our journey. I think about the countless number of African American Christian couples that do not recognize the realities of midlife crises. As I was looking for support during my journey, it became apparent to me that in Caucasian communities, Midlife Crisis (MLC) is recognized, talked about, and support groups are created. In the African American communities, not so much. While interviewing couples in preparation for this book, many African American couples didn't even recognize the term. They spoke of times when their spouses seemed to have lost their minds, spending tons of money on crazy things, or tried to recapture their youth, or had affairs.

What was happening with their spouse before the affair, before all the extra? Were there any stressors/major life changes happening prior to him/her morphing into someone you no longer recognized? The books written about MLC are usually focused on how to recognize if you are personally going through a midlife crisis. I found seven books related to midlife crisis and how it affects your marriage.

It's also important to note that this isn't about the man who has struggled with infidelity or addictions or has been irresponsible his entire life. It's just the opposite. It tends to happen more often to the husband that has always been the more responsible one. The one who always does what's best for everyone else. These are the ones that tend to struggle the most with midlife crisis.

I wrote this book because midlife crisis is real. If it is never identified and never discussed, it will continue to destroy marriages and families. The diagnosis for a marriage in the throes of MLC is dire, devastating and almost completely without hope! A marriage founded in and on the person of Jesus Christ can have a totally different diagnosis.

I wrote this book to help another spouse know that MLC does not have to be the end of their marriage but the beginning of a much better marriage. We made it, and so can they!

"Therefore, everyone who hears these words of mine and puts them into practice is like a wise man who built his house on the rock. 25 The rain came down, the streams rose, and the winds blew and beat against that house; yet it did not fall, because it had its foundation on the rock.26 But everyone who hears these words of mine and does not put them into practice is like a foolish man who built his

house on sand. 27 The rain came down, the streams rose, and the winds blew and beat against that house, and it fell with a great crash" (Matthew 7:24-27).

Please note: This is only my perspective from my experience of how we almost went to the Sunken Place. My spouse may not share my sentiments.

Part 1

"When you're young in marriage surrounded by strong pillars; Marriage mentors, intercessors and other married couples that believe in the sanctity of marriage...

It's like living in the city surrounded by tall buildings.

The wind can't get to you so easy; it can't do as much damage,

Because it's broken up before it gets to you.

However, when you move to the suburbs and leave the protection the pillars/tall buildings offer, the elements get to you much easier causing way more damage than before when the pillars/tall buildings were in place."

Gregory Sashington Sr.

Chapter 1: The Sunken Place

On the one hand, a place of change, of misunderstanding, confusion, and loneliness. On the other hand, a place of pressure cooker stress, desire to escape, confusion, feeling chained and hopeless, sometimes despair that causes you to shift your focus from a God that loves you to the disappointments in life. In marriage, this quite often looks like divorce, the place where marriages go to die.

The hurt was excruciating. My head was pounding, and my heart was beating so fast and so loud I couldn't think. My palms were sweating, and I felt dizzy. Someone was crying deep, gut-wrenching cries. I felt her cries in the depth of my soul. I wanted to reach out to her. I could not. I couldn't see. Why couldn't I see? Everything was red. My heart was beating so fast, and my mind was racing; I couldn't grab a single thought. What the hell was happening? Why can't I THINK!!! Why were my hands sweating? I can't get off the floor. Why am I on the floor? Is this what dying feels like?

What just happened? I just got hit by a Mack truck and struck by lightning. I was holding a cellphone bill that indicated, "my husband of twenty-three years, whom I love and trusted, was having some type of affair." Who was she? This could not be the woman I just asked him about, the reason I cried throughout my 44th birthday dinner. He lied to ME. We had never withheld information from each other. We had a no-drama agreement. We talked about everything.

After he was busted by a wife we had coached in the past, we talked. I asked him every question imaginable to make sure I missed nothing. He lied and lied again.

Now, I am standing here with a month-long bill worth of phone calls at one a.m., four a.m., nine a.m. to nine p.m., all throughout the day. Texts and calls, calls and texts, when I am laying right here next to him, and when I am out of town for days. Had I been foolish giving him all these years? Did he love her? Had they been together sexually? What things had he said to her to make this okay? I was losing my husband, and I had no idea.

I knew he was struggling in his Christian walk; I knew he was making bad decisions. I knew his wardrobe had upgraded and his latest choice of friends only knew how to have a good time if it involved drinking and partying in clubs. I knew he had grown cold toward me and had been resisting every attempt to be intimate. I knew my husband of twenty-plus years had changed from the man I knew and loved.

Chapter 2: Discovery

I cried the entire day of my 44th birthday. A few days before, I discovered my husband had been pretending to belong to another woman as a favor on more than one occasion.

I was at a city-wide event as a vendor for my job with my youngest daughter when I ran into a former client that my husband and I use to coach she and her husband. In the middle of the conversation, she hugs me and begins to sob uncontrollably because she ran into my husband on two occasions where he was without me. Instead, he was with another woman "pretending" to be her boyfriend at her family's event.

Blah, blah, blah I only heard bits and pieces after that. *My husband*...with someone else...pretending...who is she? What did I miss? What the hell just happened? My world was breaking, no crumbling, no crashing into pieces, and I was standing in the middle of this event with hours to go consoling her, assuring her that Greg and I would be okay.

Then, I had to drive home forty-five minutes with my youngest daughter in the car trying to keep it together.

When questioned, he lied. In a more detailed conversation, he shared the desire to experience something different. It had nothing to do with me but everything to do with me. I had become the part of his life that he was re-evaluating. The husband I loved was re-evaluating what we had. My world was officially upside down, and I didn't know what to do. I felt helpless and powerless to stop this whirlwind of negative energy that had entered this sacred space I called marriage.

Chapter 3: The Stress of It All

In 2011, After what seemed like our 1000th time, we were again rejected for a home. This was the furthest we had ever gotten in the home-buying process. Schools had been chosen, our entire apartment was packed up, and schedules and work routes had been developed, and now this. The bank decided not to go through with the loan only a week before our closing date. We were crushed.

I could not stand to think of the looks on the faces of my children. We had gone after houses before, gotten their hopes up high before, but we had never gotten this close.

The Sunday after will stay in my mind forever...

My husband and I were standing side by side in church, completely heartbroken, holding hands with tears streaming down our faces. Why weren't we acceptable enough before God to deserve a house? We faithfully served on the church Marriage Ministry for almost ten years. We were Sunday school teachers. We coached couples in our spare time. We raised our children right, to love and fear God and to do all the right things. We were givers! Why in the world did it seem like everyone in the world, sinners and unstable believers alike, get blessed with houses but not us?

That Sunday, I made an inner vow before the Lord that I would protect myself and no longer try to get a house. The hurt was too great, and I didn't think I could handle any more disappointment. That day, something shut off in my husband; apparently, he too had made an inner vow.

In 2012, my husband's work schedule increased, which led to a decrease in his attendance at church, Sunday school, and church activities. We had our first big argument in years. I started noticing a little shade being thrown every so often about my clothes and he no longer wanted to drive when we were together. On the way to a ministry cookout, he accused me of being disrespectful, of no longer caring about what he thought. I realized that my wife-dar had gotten thrown off at some point, and I had missed hints that something was wrong. I began to turn up the prayer for my husband.

During that time I could count the number of arguments we had had on one hand. I prided myself on being a good and attentive wife. We talked about just about everything. If we had a problem or felt we needed something in our marriage, we talked about it. For example, I hate wearing stockings, but Greg loves them. If he started to notice the legs of other women wearing stockings, he would share that with me, and I would wear stockings for a couple of Sundays. If we felt a certain way about someone of the opposite sex, we talked about it. However, some-where along the way this began to change for my husband.

Retirement

Greg was and will forever be a military man at heart. He was a career reservist for twenty-three years. The military had been a huge part of his life. He was in the military almost two years longer than we had been married. The military was changing. Greg began having some health challenges, and in 2012 he retired from the military.

This was no little thing, in the military, he had a brother-hood. They met regularly; he was more than a sergeant to many in his unit. He was a big brother, a counselor, and a leader. Much of who he is, is grounded in the military.

Financial Hits

Then, in 2013 some major things happen. After almost twenty years of being a stay home mom, I got a full-time job. We moved into our new home forty-five minutes from the city and my husband got a new job. I was so excited! A year of new begin-nings, what could possibly go wrong?

We had attended so many home buying workshops over the years that I guess we had become numb to all the shared infor-mation. As brand-new homeowners, we purchased our home from someone with a senior exemption. Unfortunately, we knew it would not last forever, but we forgot to keep an eye on it. Out of nowhere, our taxes increased, causing our mortgage to double.

While we struggled with our finances, our youngest daughter prepared to go away to college. In the craziness, our credit scores dropped, and we had a difficult time getting her into school. She got in, but not without Greg signing away his life in loans.

We were not prepared, and on top of that, Greg purchased both he and I new cars.

To say the least, our finances were a complete wreck. We were just trying to stay above water.

Empty Nesters

Our baby girl was leaving the nest! The entire financing for her school was a huge stressor. Nothing seemed to go our way.

Not Good Enough

The year isn't over yet. After ten years of serving in a ministry. We just knew that when the current leadership stepped down, we would be recognized for all our hard work and prayerfully be asked to assume leadership of the ministry we had loved on for over fifteen years. That did not happen. A part of me knew it would not because I had noticed the change in my husband. I knew if I saw it, Daddy God saw it long before I did. And yet, we were still deeply disappointed; I could barely process this loss because I was busy praying for the changes I was witnessing in my husband. This decision hit hard.

Chapter 4: The Way We Were

At twenty years old, I married the man of my dreams. He absolutely loved everything about me. No one could make me feel safer than Greg. One of his strengths was his willingness to become a better husband. He modeled my Dad on how to love your wife and to be gentle with her. Greg was really attentive to me, perfecting his technique of making me feel special, loved, and wanted.

Once, while we were dating, he drove almost 100 miles an hour from Mississippi to Chicago. He turned a fourteen-hour trip into a ten-hour trip with his entire family (parents and siblings) in the car, just to take me to work at 4 a.m., so I wouldn't have to catch the train by myself.

Wherever we went together, if we were apart in that place separated by hundreds of people in the same room, he was watching. If I were approached by some random guy looking to make new friends, Greg would show up out of nowhere, like a ninja. This tickled me!

Whatever we learned in our Married Couples Sunday school class, he came home and practiced making it happen. If I complained about my weight or body, he would demand I stop talking about his body because he loved it. Another man could not pull my interest because my husband was the biggest flirt towards me and my biggest admirer.

Often, I think back to the times when he just wanted to be with me. Like he really enjoyed my company. While in the military, he would have to leave for two weeks every year for training. When he would return, I could not get him off my heels. He would take a nap, and even though he was sleeping, he just wanted to have me nearby. At the time, it would drive me crazy because I would think, "He is sleeping. Why does he want me here?" He just enjoyed knowing I was close, or if he had to make a run, he would ask me to run with him. When we were away from one another, we missed each other.

My days with him on the garbage truck are some of my fondest memories. His family owned a disposal company. Occasionally, he would ask if I wanted to go to work with him. So, I would throw on one of his overly big work jumpsuits, get my sister to stay with the kids, and at 3 a.m. in the morning bounce along the streets of the westside with my husband.

I loved our date nights. I loved making love with him. I loved snuggling at night and having small talk. I loved line dancing and stepping together; we looked so good and had so much fun. I loved laughing with him over the same jokes and sharing memories. I loved teaching and discussing the Word with him. I loved encouraging him and having him pose for me in his tight military t-shirts and bulging muscles. I was his, and he was mine. I loved every minute of our life together.

After listening to the relationship horrors of his married and single friends alike, Greg would often share how very grateful he was that he'd chosen me as his wife. What we have is special. I am by no means saying either of us were perfect. But what I am saying is that we both worked very hard to make the other feel treasured and secure in our marriage. #TeamSashington.

I remember once, while in the Sunken Place, we sat in our kitchen talking during the early stages of decline. I remember our conversation about partying. With my husband's new job, new schedule, and newly found time on his hands he had been invited to all kinds of parties during the middle of the week. I remember his amazement that people were partying throughout the week.

Here's the thing about Greg and why this was so amazing. My husband is and has always been a hard worker. His work ethic is unmatched. When he was young, while other children were resting throughout the night, getting a good night's rest before a long day at school, he and his brother were up at the crack of dawn, working the back of his family's garbage truck for hours before returning home to get ready for school.

He has worked on trucks most of his life. Most of his career required super early start times. His usual schedule was for him to be in bed by eight or nine p.m. Then, he had to be up by three a.m. and out the door by four in the morning. And he worked five to six days a week. He would get off work by one or two in the afternoon, come home, nap, and spend a couple of hours with us, his wife, and kids, before repeating the cycle. He had time with his friends; however, he spent most of his time working or with family. His hanging out was saved for the weekend. This was the husband that I knew.

Chapter 5: My Superman Was Broken!

In July 2013, my sisters and I attended a pole dancing class. We had a fantastic time falling all over the place, practicing our sexy moves. We videotaped ourselves learning an incredibly sexy chair dance. I even purchased a sexy dress. I was super excited and rushed home to show my husband what I learned. I was totally expecting to be rewarded for my good efforts. My imagination danced all over the place with pictures of how this would go down. The expression on his face when he saw me in this dress would be priceless! BABY! I couldn't wait! I rushed home...to an empty house.

I texted him and told him I was on my way and that I had a surprise for him. My husband has always been a man of his word. If he says he's going to be somewhere or do something, you can put money on it. So, where was he? I set the stage, got all showered, fixed up, made up, and waited for hours. The chair dance never happened, and the dress still sits in the closet.

This was one of the early signs that something was off. There were others. For instance,

we started our family in a two-flat apartment building. Greg took care of that place as if it were his own. Our landlord loved him. We finally had our own home! I knew my husband would treat it like a castle, take care of it, maintain it, all of that. That did not happen! Things began to fall apart, and no care was given to it. He wasn't home to take care of his property the way he had taken care of someone else's.

I knew something was wrong. My husband was saying things to me he would never say. And he would say it in such a mean, spiteful, dismissive way. After he would say it, there would be a look on his face like, *"I can't believe I just said that,"* followed by, *"I don't know why I said that,"* or *"I'm sorry I said that."* And sometimes it would just be whatever came out of his mouth–with no regrets. The man that would say these things was not my husband.

He became extremely sensitive. The smallest comments from me would send him storming out of the house or into the next room. Looking back, I'm not sure if he was really being sensitive or just using it as an excuse to escape.

I remember an old female friend of his who recently entered the picture. She called him at eight or nine at night, asking him to make a run with her. He did not give it a second thought. "She needs me," he said. I almost lost it! Since when was this acceptable? Would he be so accepting if the shoe were on the other foot?

Of course not! My husband had come outside of himself! These were the type of things that were becoming commonplace in the Sunken Place. Him behaving like a single man. This was not my husband.

"You could never be my best friend!"

Greg was letting me have it! Every other day, I was being told in some way shape, or form that I was no longer what he wanted. These words hit me like daggers.

Not only could I never be his best friend, but with his introduction to Facebook, he was reconnecting with old friends and finding new friends. Most of these friendships were unhealthy; a new group of single friends led to bad decisions. We had been holding each other down for most of our adult lives. Now "I" was being replaced.

It's Your Fault

Suddenly, everything was my fault. Our finances were in ruins, my fault. The house was falling apart, my fault. He was not free to live his "best life," my fault. Mind you, we made all our decisions together, but in the Sunken Place, everything was my fault.

Got to make a quick run. Making a quick stop after work, etc.

I've absolutely grown to hate these phrases. These became code words for *"Don't wait up, I'm going to be awhile."* The curfew we had given ourselves before, if we were hanging out with our friends was 2 a.m. In the sunken place rarely did he make it home before curfew. There was always a reason why he couldn't be home on time.

We'll see...

Prior to this season, we made space for one another. We would check in with one another before making plans. Now, none of his plans included me. When I'd try to schedule something with our mutual friends or families, it was always, "We'll see." His time was reserved for his friends.

Can't Be Bothered

Because we respected each other, if we called each other and the call was missed, we would call right back. If one of us sent a text, we responded quickly. In this season of our lives, if I texted him, my text would go unanswered. When asked about it, he actually said to me, "I saw your text. I just didn't feel like being bothered."

My Biggest Critic

Nothing I wore was acceptable. V-necks were too low, dresses too short or see through, the bra too thin. I mean, everything I wore was critiqued. I remember inviting him to go with me on a work trip. The drive was about three hours away. I was so excited, looking forward to some alone time with him. I wore this cute little sporty type of dress with my little silver accessories, thinking, "Gurl, you fine! He is going to love you in this dress!"

Nope. He spent the entire ride angry at me and utterly disgusted with my choice of travel clothes. I was floored. It put a damper on our whole trip. This happened on multiple occasions, no matter what I wore. Whenever I dressed up cute, he would find a reason to get upset and ruin the evening.

Secret Bank Accounts

As long as we've been married, we always had shared accounts. In the Sunken Place, he had a separate account. Not only didn't I know about it, I also wasn't listed on it.

The Silent Treatment

If we went places together, the trip there and the trip home was in silence. If we were having a good time, all it took was a perceived look by me, or if I disagreed with him, our situation would be shut down, followed by the silent treatment for the rest of the night. This became my punishment when he wasn't happy with something I said or did.

Please Don't Touch Me!

The minute we finished having sex, he hurried to the bathroom to clean himself. It was never that way before! Now, I imagined him scrubbing the feel of me, the scent of me off him.

Gone were the days of snuggling, sweet talk, and kisses after making love.

This is what twenty-plus years of marriage had become. I am lying in bed with him, and he is literally hanging on to his side of the bed, as if I disgust him. He acts like the thought of me, the sight of me, the smell of me turns his stomach. I cry myself to sleep. It is not the first night; it's most nights for at least the next few years.

How much longer can I live like this? How do I not take this personal? My heart breaks a little more every day. This behavior was so out of character for him. These were the little reminders that something was incredibly wrong. My Superman was broken.

Chapter 6: Killing Sista Gurl Again

My husband and I ran the activities committee for the married couple's ministry for a mega-church for almost ten years. Each year, we oversaw over 200 couples for a marriage getaway for Valentine's weekend.

For years we were a well-oiled machine, ministering to other couples on this romantic weekend. Every year, on the last day of the getaway, we would gather with some of our friends and chill. We would enjoy the fruit of our labor, relax, and share testimonies. Sometimes it was as simple as catching a show or staying an extra night just to chill. Without fail, when we got home, we would nap or snuggle and catch up on shows.

This year was different! I noticed he had not been as tuned in this year. On the way home, he shared with me that he wasn't staying home. He was going to kick it with the guys. I was a little shocked, to say the least. I remember asking if any females were going to be there, so perhaps I could join him. "Naw, it's just the guys," he said.

So, imagine my surprise when I scrolled down Facebook and there was a picture of my husband in a compromising, inappropriate position with some chick! It was the first night, we ever slept in separate beds, in separate rooms, in the same house.

The damage was done! Anyone who knows me "pre-Jesus," KNOWS I struggle with an alter-ego. I call her Sista Gurl. Sista Gurl (my flesh) does not know the definition of a kind word. Her role models were Susan Lucci, Rosanne, Diahann Carroll, and Joan Collins. She was sarcastic, condescending, and unnecessarily mean. She used her words like a knife, and anyone could get it!

On this day as she was sleeping soundly, that Facebook pic kicked the door wide open! Sista Gurl was wide awake and ready to be tagged in! That night we slept in separate rooms. The next morning was the beginning of the most hellish time of my marriage.

Now, not only was I trying to survive and make sense of what was happening with my husband, but I was also back to killing Sista Gurl! In past years, she had been my toughest competitor. Her words always hit below the belt. She always went for the jugular; she's used to drawing blood, causing harm.

The trust was completely wrecked. I searched his Facebook pages, his drawers, pockets, and phone for proof of his infidelity. This became a daily fight. Should I trust and rest in Daddy's ability to fix, deliver, and heal or take matters into my own hands (which doesn't usually work out very well) and let Sista Gurl have her way? I found myself doing everything I had coached wives *not* to do.

I wish I had the words to describe the torture I felt struggling daily to put Sista Gurl in a chokehold. Although I thought I killed her initially, apparently I only put her to sleep, and this thing was literally wearing me out. Being placed back in this predicament through no fault of my own, only served to piss me off more.

Sista Gurl was relentless. Every little thing became a trigger for me. I labeled everything my husband said or did, as a lie. Nights were sometimes just torturous, tossing and turning, lying on my side of the bed crying. Some days, I felt bombarded by the thoughts of him with other women and not wanting me. Confused, feeling like I was losing my mind, I began to seriously question whether the first twenty years of my marriage was as great as I thought.

To say I was embarrassed was an understatement. Who saw Greg while he was out, pretending to be someone else, living someone else's life? I worried about what people thought about me, him, our marriage. We used to be the model couple, that couple that others wanted to be like. We encouraged and coached couples through difficult times in marriage. Suddenly, my husband was doing all the things we encouraged couples not to do.

I just wanted to kill him. I wanted him to hurt like I hurt. There were days I cried because my Sista Gurl (my flesh) and the Spirit of God in me were playing tug of war. Sista Gurl wanted to smash the windows out of his car and burn up all his newly bought clothes. Yet, the Holy Spirit kept encouraging me to trust Him.

On cue, Sista Gurl did not come empty-handed. She brought with her temptation and more temptation. My inboxes on Facebook Messenger and Words with Friends began to fill up with men telling me all the things I wanted to hear from my husband. How beautiful I was, how they would love to get to know me. Cute, flirtatious conversations ensued. It felt so good to be noticed, to be wanted, even if it was superficially. A crush I had from years ago resurfaced, out of the blue, with great conversation, some Word, and a listening ear. That little Sista Gurl demon is crafty.

I heard my very good friend and brother Greg Cox saying, when he and his wife were going through, he would remind himself that "he did not want his wife to have to step over any bodies when she returned." I was done. It kept me from going where Sista Gurl was encouraging me to go.

The gracious spirit-filled side of me wanted to forgive him so we could return to normal, wanted to be understanding, prayerful, and patiently waiting for Daddy to deliver my husband. Ugh! I cried so many tears of frustration.

Thankfully, I had allowed the love of God to so completely consume me that Sista Gurl did not stand a chance. If she had her way, I would have caved. I would have done all the things that made my flesh feel good, even though it would have only been a temporary pleasure.

Chapter 7: Déjà Vu

U gh! I hate it here!! How did I get here again? From 2003 until 2004, my husband served in Operation Enduring Freedom in Iraq for almost a year and a half. When he returned home for nearly three years, I felt like I did not have a husband. I was utterly alone.

I eagerly awaited his return home, desperately missing him. First, nobody told me what to expect when he returned home. I simply was not prepared for the outburst, the angriness, the mood swings, and sensing that he did not want to be with me. He wanted his military buddies because they understood his struggle, and I had absolutely no clue. No clue of what he experienced, what he saw, what he felt. The anger he struggled to hold back. I simply would not understand. I was never given the opportunity or the choice to understand. He simply chose his army family.

Eventually, I realized it was not his fault. I was able to pray and google how best to support him during this time. I certainly did not understand Grace or rest. I could only identify with the hurt. Here we were in another major crisis where my husband was struggling, and I had to, again, make the decision to stand my ground as his loving wife and support him. I was frankly sick of this! When would I get a chance to crack and have him hold me down? Was our whole marriage meant to be about my husband being able to do whatever he wanted to do and me having to hold him down and support him? I was so over it!

Looking back, I now understand that both incidents were related to Mental Health. That didn't make it hurt any less. I remember having a meltdown moment with my friend and marriage mentor, Marie. I was having a full-on Sista Gurl moment and making a decision to spend the night away from home. My reasoning was I didn't know what he was doing with his free time, and he didn't need to know what I was doing with mine.

I struggled with figuring out where to go. I had a name and a place. I wanted him to hurt. Oh, how I wanted him to worry about me. I wanted him to be concerned when he came home to an empty house. I wanted him to know that someone found me beautiful, desirable, and sexy.

Anyway, back to my meltdown. I was pissed, and I remember saying to Marie, "Why do I have to be his cheerleader all of the time? When does he get to be mine?"

Marie said something that night that shut me down. She said, "Sarita, he wasn't created for you. You were created for him."

I totally received what she said. However, I still didn't go home that night. I reached out to a friend I trusted not to judge me or Greg, and I stayed at her house for the night. The next day we made up, and for the first time in months, he held me while we slept.

I am grateful that the Lord gave me the desire to fill myself with the Word. Because I was full of the Word, Sista Gurl didn't have the same power she had in the early days of my marriage. The Word simply won out!

Chapter 8: The Loneliness of It All

Here's the thing. We were teen parents. So, when our last baby left the nest, we were in our early forties. My thoughts were like, Yesss! Time to TURN ALL THE WAY UP! Me and my man! Baby, we 'bout to get it! Hanging out, traveling, doing whatever we were big and bad enough to do...Together!

And then there was nothing. How did we get here? I mean honestly the years prior to this were amazing. I loved my husband; he was my best friend. Suddenly, I was being pushed to the side and replaced by old friends and new friends who were introduced into our lives via Facebook. I wasn't enough anymore.

In 2010, I went back to school. Prior to that I had some good friends that served in the ministry with us. I remember when the wife went back to school, her husband came to every event alone. This went on for about a good two years. I remember thinking, *"Wow, that's a dangerous place to be. So, tied up with school that your spouse is left alone all the time to their own devices."*

I'm pretty sure this was playing in the back of my mind when I went back to school. We were both working at the time. I dragged my laptop to every home get-together. My husband hooked up with old friends and began hanging out on the weekends. Greg would say, "Babe, you coming?"

I would have to respond, "I can't! I have to finish this paper, maybe next time."

Lounges and clubs weren't schoolwork friendly. This was the only pastime for this group of people. Soon it was no longer just the weekends. The hanging out began happening throughout the week. He would leave for work at 4 a.m., and I would not see him again until much later in the evening. It wasn't long before the nights grew longer and longer, 11 p.m. turned into midnight, then, 2 a.m., 3 a.m.....

I was never lonelier than when I was home alone, scrolling through Facebook, besieged with pics of other couples, spending time together, looking as though they enjoyed each other's company. Or, when husbands would profess their dying love for their spouse or post pics celebrating their wives' beauty. Is there another word for deep loneliness? Extreme loneliness?

While my husband was enjoying his unexcused extended hall pass, I was home alone.

Being alone and neglected brought back memories and feelings of those reminiscent of when he returned from the war in Iraq. I mentioned I struggled with infidelity early in our marriage. The enemy's attack was full-blown, and Sista Gurl was struggling to make a comeback.

Night after night, several times a night I would walk to the front door or the office window looking for his truck in the driveway. Did I mention I was experiencing extreme loneliness?

Part II

Cause I'm broken

Down to nothing

But I'm still holding on to the one thing

You are God

You are strong when

I am weak

I can do all things

through Christ who gives me strength

And I don't have to be

strong enough

strong enough

Strong Enough by Matthew West

Chapter 9: The Year of Restoration

*Restoration is not a sprint, It's a marathon, long, grueling and,
painful with small victories along the way.*

Pastor Joseph Prince announced the theme given to him
by the Lord as 2015, the Year of Restoration! Yaaaasss! I
receive that! Finally, Daddy was going to save my marriage from the mess it had become and restore it to its former
glory. Perhaps, even better than before. I was soooo off base! I
had no idea how restoration works. So, imagine my surprise
when it looked like my husband was getting worse, not better.

Before the discovery of the affair, there were times we still
laughed together or had sex. Every waking moment wasn't excruciating. Now, there were just too many of the excruciating days
and not enough of the other.

Some very interesting things began to happen simultane-
ously. On the one hand, Greg's secret was out, and he was pissed.
To further punish me, he withdrew even more. He never

complimented me anymore. Every time I posed question, he answered with an attitude. We argued! Boy, did we argue! Every car ride was in silence. Whenever he was with me or around family, he kept his phone in his hand. When we took a road trip, we slept in separate beds. I was left just shaking my head.

Greg was angry, grumpy, selfish, dismissive, disrespectful, overly sensitive, and just overall dissatisfied with our life. I remember thinking, Daddy, if this is restoration, you can keep it!

Chapter 10: Layers

Daddy began removing layers. In the spirit, I could see them falling off. I can't explain it. It was like watching the gardener prune a tree, removing the dead leaves, and watching them fall. If the dead leaves are not removed, the tree will never become healthy.

It started after we attended a church Valentine's retreat for married couples with a few friends. During one of the sessions where we were all together (husbands and wives), one of the presenters shared his story of getting too close to a female co-worker, which turned into an affair. He also shared how he and his wife survived and overcame his infidelity together.

I WAS STUNNED!! Here we were, Greg and me sitting together in this place just two short months since discovering his own infidelity. This man was telling our story! I was done! SOOO amazed at what the Lord was doing. I was overwhelmed with emotion. I dare not cry in front of Greg. Tears from me during this time only frustrated and aggravated him. So, I ran to the bathroom to have my moment. While there, I cried out to Daddy that He would help Greg to forgive himself.

Daddy forgave his sin years ago at the cross. I had chosen to forgive him before it was revealed. Having had my own indiscretion years ago, I knew how guilt, shame, and condemnation could eat you alive. I did not want my husband to experience that torture.

As I returned to the table, the husband was continuing his story. He went on to say that God had forgiven him, and his wife had forgiven him. But the hardest part was forgiving himself, but eventually, he was able to do just that.

I was in awe of how Daddy God had answered my prayer! It was the best setup EVER!

The Second Time Stays Fresh on my Mind

About a year or so after discovery, I was blessed to sit on a community committee with a Bishop who pastored a church. At some point, I was led to ask if he had ever experienced midlife crisis. To my surprise, he answered yes and began to share his story with me.

A few months later, the Holy Spirit led me to host a workshop on Avoiding the Sunken Place. Greg and I were just out of the discovery stage. We weren't even sure we still liked each other, and yet Daddy God was calling me to host a workshop on Avoiding the Sunken Place when I wasn't even sure we had avoided the Sunken Place.

I dragged my feet for months. Daddy laid on my heart the name of a sister in Christ who is a mental health expert who could collaborate with me on this project. I hesitated. I didn't want to seem as though I was taking her for granted. There were a thousand reasons why I didn't want to reach out to her. They all had to do with me dragging my feet. A few months later, I woke up in the wee hours of the morning with a very clear directive from Daddy to call her that day. When I called her, she confirmed what I had heard. Daddy God had also awakened her in the wee hours, told her I was going to call, and that she was to collaborate with me on this project. The format consisted of Midlife Crisis from a mental health expert, testimony from the Bishop, and small group conversation.

In preparation, I told my husband about the vision Daddy God had given me. For months, I tried to reassure Greg that it wasn't about making him look bad but instead about helping other couples that might find themselves in a similar predicament. Over and over again, I shared with him that I would leave space for him on the agenda to share whatever he felt led to share.

The event was amazing! We sold out of our tickets. Interestingly enough, few showed up. However, the success wasn't based on how many people showed or didn't show. It was about the testimony of a strong black family man, a leader in his church sharing from a very vulnerable place as he told his own personal struggle with midlife crisis. As he spoke, it was as if he had been living in our home the last few months. It seemed as if he was saying all the things *my* husband felt but couldn't voice. If no one had shown up, I knew the mission had been accomplished.

Hearing this man's testimony was exactly what my husband needed, to see and hear someone who looked like him, someone in a leadership position, to know and understand he wasn't alone. He wasn't an oddity; this could happen to anyone. For me, the Bishop's words inspired hope and healing.

My husband also decided to speak. He shared how he had gotten caught up. How he had "sworn to protect me from enemies both foreign and domestic; some kind of way he had become the enemy." Never in a million years would I have imagined him sharing publicly any part of his story. My mind was BLOWN! Our God is good, and His mercy endures forever! Daddy was continuously removing layers. I moved as I was led, and Daddy did what was needed.

Another pivotal moment was when I was admitted into the hospital with double pneumonia and pericarditis. Pericarditis is when the sac around your heart becomes filled with an excessive amount of fluid, and it begins to restrict the function of your heart. My husband spent every day with me in the hospital. He would stop by before and after work and stayed all day on the weekends. This was important because all his spare time was usually spent with his friends.

The weekend after I was admitted, was a huge annual picnic day with Greg's favorite group of friends. Every year, he committed yearly to spending sunup to sundown hanging out with them. However, this Saturday he stopped by the picnic, and then spent the rest of the day at the hospital with me. He chose me!

It's been three years, and tonight he chose me again! After five days of traveling, I came home Thursday night and was greeted by a husband who was ready for lovemaking. Friday morning, we woke, ate breakfast, watched a show, and went back to bed together. We woke, went to dinner, and went to our friend's house party where we laughed, danced drank, and were good.

Saturday morning, I woke to the sound of my husband calling me baby and gently massaging my thigh, reminding me that it was time for work. We met after work for a friend's birthday bowling party. Ladies were asked to wear red, men black. My only red shirt said Brewer on the back. He insisted and switched out my shirt for a white one that said Sashington. I wore it gladly! Choosing me was beginning to happen more and more.

The layers were falling off! Yet, between the removal of layers was pure torture mainly because I was so anxious for our marriage to be refreshed, to get my husband back, to not hurt anymore, and to feel his continuous love for me.

There were little ways Daddy allowed me to see him working behind the scenes.

Chapter 11: Sprinkles of Grace

Through all this, Greg was supportive. He was supportive of my speaking engagements, supportive of my mom moving in, supportive of Daddy's Favorite Ministry events. He even said to me, "I hoped you know that I will always support you."

There were moments...we binge-watched several TV series and attended church together every Sunday. For every business trip, he drove me to the airport, walked with me to the gate, and prayed with me before sending me off. When I returned, he also picked me up. These times together were the highlights of this season for me. It was one of the ways I got to spend quality time with him. I cherished every moment.

I was also led to share the Joseph Prince daily devotional with him. Every morning before he left for work or on our way to the airport, I would read aloud the devotion for that day.

A few times, I brought up the subject of possible counseling to my husband; of course, he rejected that idea. But God! It turns out military veterans have certain substantial benefits available to them for serving in the war. My husband was encouraged by a friend to pursue his benefits. Guess what one of the requirements was to receive the benefits? You guessed it! Counseling. My Daddy God loves him some Greg and Sarita!

I remember asking Greg if he noticed a change happening within himself. Of course, he said no. (I knew he would). He was not in a place to notice anything. I asked anyway because the Holy Spirit was blowing my mind!

I could tell when a layer had fallen because Greg became softer and gentler with me. He began to look and sound like the man I married. Under the layers were the practices we started years ago to keep our marriage safe. Things like him sharing his whereabouts with me, answering my texts, letting me know when he was on his way, and coming home when he said he would, sharing his day with me, and his truck in our driveway.

Chapter 12: He Kept Me

When going through difficult times in your marriage, it's so easy to focus on all the things your spouse is or isn't doing. "If it weren't for my spouse..." It's easier to focus on him instead of what you could be doing to stay sane, strong, hopeful, etc. I get it. He's the source of the pain. The days I took my focus off Daddy and instead focused on my husband's antics, were the very days I yearned to kill him.

Let me share the miraculous things that happened when I made Daddy God my focus.

He kept me. There are four very distinct ways He kept me because I was incapable of keeping myself.

First, right around the time things started to fall apart, my daughter's car broke down. At the same time, she had just started a job working nights. With her evening work schedule, she needed my car to get back and forth to work. During this same time, my husband decided to ghost me.

Let me just say I am not as saved as I would like to believe. We have survived adultery in our marriage in the early years, me being the offender. When my hubby returned from a year's tour in Iraq, I spent about three years yearning for the man that left to return. The one who missed and loved me and wanted to spend time with me, instead of his army buddies.

Having my husband again choose his friends over me was hurtful.

Having a vehicle would have presented me with way too many opportunities to repeat history, way too many opportunities to get revenge to hurt him like he was hurting me. My daughter needed my car. This kept me out of trouble, and from having an even bigger mess to clean up. Daddy God kept me when I wasn't trying to keep myself.

Sashingtoned

In my profession as a trainer, I traveled across the country training clients on how to implement our curriculum. During our Sunken Place season, every trip ended with my flight home being canceled or delayed for no apparent reason. It happened so often that one of my bosses coined the term "you've been Sashingtoned."

Here's the deal, although I was Sashingtoned. Each time was an adventure. I had the most amazing experiences whale watching in Oregon, hill climbing in San Francisco, participating in an old school car parade in Springfield, Mo., exploring the mountains of Muir Forest, discovering waterfalls and zip-lined in Tennessee to name a few. I saw and did things I probably would have never done. It was a blessing, because based on what was happening at home, I wasn't rushing to go home to be alone with my thoughts.

As we moved towards healing, being Sashingtoned happened less and less. He kept me.

Daddy's Favorite Ministry

It is the grace of God to give me a place to turn my attention to when my better half is out of control. I cannot stress enough how important it is to NOT focus on the behavior of your spouse. Instead, I encourage you to set your sight on Jesus alone. In all His wisdom, Daddy dropped in my spirit the need to share grace with just about anyone that would listen. I began to do this by starting a not-for-profit "Daddy's Favorite Ministry-Transforming Relationships through Grace." Every Monday for four years via Facebook Live, I encouraged both believers and nonbelievers to embrace the unapologetic, fullness of Daddy God's unadulterated grace.

Daddy God knows how to set me up. While I set out to encourage others, the result was that I encouraged myself. As I prepared each weekly message, I was reminded of things like how much Daddy God loves me. How He freely gives me all things, how He is a healer and deliverer, how He is victorious, and so am I. These truths helped center me. Sharing in this way blessed me in more ways than even I could imagine.

Church Home

Until we attended the retreat, I had never visited the church that hosted that event. When I walked into the retreat, there was a former principal from my grammar school. She was so excited to see me. She had received a prayer card with my name and had been praying for me. I told her I had never submitted a card, thank God for whoever submitted that card on my behalf.

Afterward, I realized this was the same church calling me and offering to pray with me saying they had received a card with my name asking for prayer. I had never visited this church. Thanks to my mom and Grandma, I was taught to listen to the Holy Spirit and follow where He leads. I felt the Holy Spirit leading us to a new church.

Attending church with my husband every Sunday allowed me to witness Daddy God working on our behalf as He ministered to both of us. The messages are focused on "grace." The Pastors often refer to God as Daddy. They also acknowledged and addressed mental health. My husband and I went up multiple times for prayer, something we would have never done in our former church for fear of what people might think. After years of ministering to others, we were now being ministered to in a different way. Desperate times called for desperate measures, and it was time to let Daddy out of the box we had created for Him.

The delivery was different. The music was contemporary Christian; however, we loved gospel music. This was a medium-sized church; we were coming from a megachurch. At this church, we knew very few people; at our former church, we knew almost everyone. So many things were vastly different, but the Word was ROCK SOLID.

For about a year, based on his work schedule, we traveled between churches attending either Saturday evenings at one church or Sunday mornings at the other. Eventually, we just stuck to the one. The thing I missed most was discussing the messages after church. It was by far the best part of my Sunday, sharing highlights from the sermons each Sunday with our children and with one another. In the Sunken Place, that wasn't even an option. Yet, I knew Daddy was working. He's so good at keeping me!

Part III

In the eye of the storm

He remains in control

In the middle of the war

You guard my soul

You alone are the anchor

When my sails are torn

Your love surrounds me

In the eye of the storm

Eye of the Storm by Ryan Stevenson

Chapter 13: In the Eye of the Storm

While on a flight with a friend, I fell asleep. Sometime during the flight, we hit some nasty turbulence. The plane dipped and shook violently several times, causing my friend to shout out loud, grab me, and call on the name of Jesus. It was scary! The first dip woke me; then it startled me. My first thought was Jesus!!!! My second thought was I'm on the plane, meaning right now, there's absolutely no way out of this situation. I don't control any facets of this wild ride.

When I'm in situations that make me feel helpless, hopeless, worried, afraid, out of control, I remind myself that "Oh, Daddy's Got Me." We prayed for our safety before the flight, and there was nothing I could do. I could not control the situation, so the best thing for me to do was to continue to rest. So, I went back to sleep. I returned to my place of rest.

The eye of the storm is usually the worse part of any storm. Before the discovery, we were taking it one day at a time; it was tolerable. After discovery, all hell broke out! I have a defense mechanism that kicks into high gear whenever I feel over-whelmed or afraid. I run straight to Daddy, to His presence, His Word, His promises. He became the very air I breathe. My day started and ended with Him. In the wee hours of the morning, I spent quiet time with Him. I literally could not start my day with-out first spending time in His presence.

Being in the Sunken Place was very much like being in the eye of the storm. The situation was completely out of my control. I hope this book will not only give you hope but will also help you recognize some of the signs that you or your spouse might be headed to or are already in the Sunken Place (Midlife Crisis).

Chapter 14: Sunken Place Triggers

How does one get to this Sunken Place? What pushes a person to the point of becoming someone they no longer recognize? What triggers the Sunken Place?

Triggers can be but are not limited to:

Retirement

It is the reality of being connected to a place, the people, the camaraderie, the routine, and the comfortability of that place. What it represents to you, the place of importance you gave it in your life is all gone after a significant amount of time—a place where most people have worked for as long as twenty-plus years.

Health Issues

As we get to the middle of our lives, we may begin to experience more health issues. These health issues can cause us to face our mortality and make some hard lifestyle choices. Our friends start dying. Our parents begin dying. We may feel helpless, hopeless, and out of control.

Financial Pressures

Major financial pressures can come when a family transitions from an apartment to a house, taking on overwhelming financial responsibilities. Additional challenges occur when you have children in college, student debt, foreclosures, repossessions, and personal loans. The list can go on if there is a constant barrage of financial difficulties. All of this can become overwhelming and depressing.

Empty Nesters

Children grow up and leave your home. Often times, couples don't spend enough time getting to know each other during the time they're raising their children. Once the children are gone, one or both parents may experience loneliness or emptiness without their children. Being a parent can consume a person's identity in such a way that when the children leave home, the parent feels lost and begins to wander; sometimes that wandering, that feeling of not being anchored to anything, leads to a downward spiral. This is also a time when couples realize they are no longer as connected as they once were.

Sunken Place Quiz (Please circle one)

1. Do you feel cheated by life? Do you feel like you haven't gotten what you think you deserve for all your hard work? Yes or No

2. Does your spouse seem like he/she is trying to relive his/her younger days? Yes or No

3. Are you feeling dissatisfied with life, like you want to experience something different? Yes or No

4. Do you feel overwhelmingly selfish most of the time? Yes or No

5. In the last three to five years, have you experienced a series of major disappointments? Yes or No

6. Is your spouse behaving like a completely different person? Yes or No

7. Do you feel confused about what you're feeling? Yes or No

8. Is your spouse spending unusual amounts of time away from home? Yes or No

9. Is it difficult to communicate what's going on with you to your spouse? Yes or No

10. Has your personal prayer time with Daddy and/or church attendance significantly decreased? Yes or No

11. Have you experienced a major life change in the last three to five years, such as career change, becoming empty nesters, financial pressure, health issues, etc.? Yes or No

12. Do you feel angry most of the time? Yes or No

13. Has your appetite changed? Yes or No

14. Is he/she struggling with insomnia or sleeping way too much? Yes or No

15. Does your spouse seem extremely worried about their health and have frequent doctor's visits, etc.? Yes or No

If you answered yes to seven or more questions, you and or your spouse could be headed for the "Sunken Place!"

Chapter 15: If Your Spouse is in the Sunken Place

Realize that although it may feel personal, it is not. Recognize the fight is not with your spouse...

1. It's spiritual, not physical (Ephesians 6:12).

2. It's not your fight (2 Chronicles 20:15).

3. Pray without ceasing for your spouse (James 5:16).

Applying these scriptures gave me life morning after morning when I woke with my husband heavy on my heart. God's Word helped me to see my husband as not only my husband but my brother in Christ. He was in desperate need of prayer. I'm his wife, bone of his bone, and flesh of his flesh. His helpmeet, the only woman anointed to go to war on his behalf. In this area, I am uniquely empowered to stand in the gap for my husband. No one will speak life to his situation the way I can and will. When I became his wife, I received an anointing to have his back.

The enemy had developed his plan, strategized, and launched an attack against me and my husband and our marriage to thwart

Daddy's plan for his life. My husband couldn't see it. His vision during this time had become blurred by life's disappointments. I am his partner in the field with more experience in warring with the enemy. So, I was able to see the attack in action and gear up.

I have an analogy I often used when referring to marriage. When I attended camp as a young girl, we had a buddy system whenever we went swimming. This meant we could not swim alone. If something happened, my buddy would be aware and help me or call for help and support me in getting back to a safe space. For example, if I got a leg cramp or a strong undercurrent caught me off guard, I wouldn't be alone. Most importantly, we wore our life jackets which were designed to prevent us from drowning. Now, I didn't say you wouldn't go under. I said you wouldn't drown. The life jackets were the sure way to bring you back up when you were pulled underwater.

Marriage is exactly like that, a buddy system. If you are a believer, you and your spouse have a supernatural life jacket called the Holy Spirit. If a strong current catches your spouse off guard and temporarily pulls him or her under, have no doubt you will both go under. The saving grace is your life jacket, the Holy Spirit. Although you go under, God will not leave you there. He will propel you out of the water, out of the darkness towards the light, ensuring your return to a safe place.

Chapter 16: Firm Foundation

One of the greatest lessons I learned early in my Christian walk was to have quiet time with Daddy God. During prayer or reading His word, or quietly listening to praise and worship, I was encouraged to listen for His voice. For some reason, that whole being still and quiet before God, waiting to hear from Him, never really worked for me. As a mom with young children, anytime I sat still and quiet, I would fall asleep! Ironically, I heard Him the most while I was washing dishes or cleaning the kitchen. Usually, this occurred in the wee hours of the morning or late at night when the house was quiet. I'd hear Him the most when my spirit was quiet and focused on His love for me. During the worse chapter of the Sunken Place, I needed to hear from God every day. Otherwise, I would have been out! This was one of the most important tools in the arsenal of believing Daddy God for my marriage.

Around 2008 or so, while on bed rest after surgery, I encountered Joseph Prince's ministry. Pastor Prince taught me powerful lessons of Grace, Identity, and Rest. These were biblical foundations I stood on as I believed God for my marriage.

Grace
Crazy, Ridiculous, Unmerited Favor

My entire faith journey, my understanding of Grace, was a kind of watered-down description of God's riches at Christ's Expense. In my heart, I felt like it was more than that, richer than that. However, the people around me didn't seem to have the answer. Eventually, I found myself in a bad space. I was a Sunday school teacher, ministry leader, and wife coach who really loved God. Yet, I found myself in a very unhealthy space. I struggled for more years than I care to admit. I was lonely, confused, tortured, tired, and some days felt completely hopeless.

I would promise myself not today and fail. I would cry out to God, "Why won't you deliver me?" After a while, I started to question whether this sin was the real me. Then, came this revelation of Grace. In the midst of my madness, Daddy God was loving on me. I was so undeserving, and yet HE continued to bless and keep me with no judgment because of the blood. By the grace of God, when He looks at me, He does not see the sins of Sarita but the blood of Christ. So, when He looks at me, He sees the finished product. This same grace motivated me to see the finished product of my husband, to see the righteousness of Christ on Him, the same way Daddy God saw it on me. It also had equipped me to stand and minister grace to my husband the same way it had been ministered to me.

Identity

*God made Him who had no sin to be sin for us, so that in Him
we might become the righteousness of God (2 Cor 5:21 NIV).*

During this revelation, I was introduced to new verses that
showed me as a believer, I was not my sin. "I am the righteousness
of God through Christ". I was reminded that "As He is so am I
in this world" *(1 John 4:17 KJV),* in every sense of the word. I am
righteous, delivered, forgiven, redeemed, healed, perfected forever, completely accepted in Christ, highly favored, and deeply
loved by HIM. Christ is my identity.

The more I meditated on and focused on my standing with
Daddy God, the sooner the chains fell off. I wasn't trapped anymore. I embraced this new level of intimacy with Daddy. I felt so
relieved, free, and extremely grateful. I needed to share this new
covenant grace with every believer; every believer who is bogged
down with all the don'ts and "rules" of Christianity unable to enjoy their relationship with Daddy.

Anyway, this new identity is what I took with me into the
Sunken Place. The confidence of knowing that Daddy wasn't
holding anything against me. And this didn't have anything to do
with Karma. All things were working for our good because
Daddy loved both Greg and I individually and collectively. I
am/we are victorious because Christ is victorious!

Rest

"When you work, God rests, When God works, you rest" - *Joseph Prince.*

This concept is not one of inactivity but of Holy Spirit-led/directed activity. It speaks to Daddy being in control of all situations, including yours. It speaks to His big picture vision for your life, which is far greater than whatever you had imagined for your life.

It speaks to a Father's love for His child; He doesn't want me to be stressed out or worried about the outcome of anything. But instead, He wants me to rest on His finished work at the cross. At the cross, His rest became my rest. What helped me to rest, was knowing that my relationship with Daddy God was based on what I believed about Him. I couldn't and did not compare His relationship with His other children to my unique relationship with Him.

This is important to note: when I discovered and researched MLC, almost 95% of marriages caught in the throes of MLC end in divorce. The underlying message implied, "There was nothing I could do. I had to let it run its course." I refused to let that be the end of our story. Based on my relationship with Daddy God, regardless of what I saw happening to other marriages of unbelievers and believers alike, I was determined to stand for my marriage, and stand firmly on what I believed about Him.

Every relationship is different. People bring different experiences into their relationships, different beliefs, hurts, baggage, etc. These beliefs, these experiences, shape what our relationship with Daddy God looks like and whether He will save our marriage. If I had compared our situation to the situations of others, it would have taken me down. Why? Because I would have based it on information like, "This couple was a Christian powerhouse, and they didn't make it, how can we?" Or "It takes both people to stand for the marriage."

I don't know if they know how much Daddy God loves them. I don't know if they have a confident expectation of good because of His love for them. I don't know if they believe all their sins are forgiven, past, present, and future. I don't know if they see themselves the way Daddy sees them...*the righteousness of God through Christ Jesus (2 Cor 5:21 NIV)*. I don't know if they know how to rightly divide the word of truth. I don't know if they operate under the law, "Do bad, get bad. Do good, get good," or under grace (He richly gave us all things at the cross). I don't know.

Instead, I rested on what I do know, "I will not fear, for it is His great pleasure to give me the Kingdom "*(Luke 12:32 KJV)*. It refreshes Him to bless me. He loves my husband and me. He loves marriage. He isn't holding anything against me. He isn't angry with me. I am not waiting for the other shoe to drop where He's concerned. It isn't dropping. "He can do exceedingly and abundantly above all I can ask or imagine" *(Eph 3:20 KJV)*. All His promises to me are yes and amen.

"As He is so am I in this world" *(1 John 4:17 KJV)*. If Christ is victorious, then so am I! "Finally, brothers and sisters whatever is true, whatever is noble, whatever is right, whatever pure, whatever is lovely, whatever is admirable, if anything is excellent or praiseworthy and of good report think on these things" *(Phil 4:8 NIV)*.

Standing on these principles gave me rest and the ability to stand when I wanted to give up. At the cross, it was determined that all things were working for my good! At the cross was where my victory was won, not just for a few of my troubles, but for all my troubles! At the cross, the result was good through eternity.

Just prior to the Sunken Place, I was practicing the Art of Resting. Daddy led us to not one, but two victories. Even though we had little to no money, we made the tumultuous, crazy purchase of our home. And we were able to see our son's successful graduation from a Historically Black College and University (HBCU). I understand now that those were small tests of faith to prepare me for one of the biggest tests of my marriage and my life.

Chapter 17: Friends are Everything

It is so very tempting to talk about and or complain about what you see. However, the Word of God reminds us that the power of life and death is in our tongue. Everyone needs to vent from time to time, especially when they're going through. However, when you're venting, processing, or reflecting, be sure the person you're speaking to is safe, a trusted confidante. Not only should they keep your confidence, but they should also be spiritually mature enough to:

1. Listen objectively and respectfully without judgment or bias

2. Be comfortable with silence, allowing you the space to vent without interjecting and providing unwanted advice

3. Gently point you back to Daddy God, not in a teaching kind of way.

Does that seem strange? It once seemed strange to me as well. I used to think, who talks like that? How is that even possible?

Here's how it worked for me: my sister and I talked daily about a program we both watched each morning—the Joseph Prince Ministry broadcast. We would laugh and exclaim Daddy's love for us and embrace the Word of God as it was being unveiled to us– this mystery of Grace. Wherever I found myself with my spouse in the Sunken Place and needed a safe space to vent, cry, process, and someone to pray with me and for me, I found it in my single sister. She would quickly remind me of Daddy's word towards me. Often, it was something we had just learned that morning, like "I wasn't fighting *for* victory but from the victory that was won for me at the cross.

Sometimes she would mimic our mom as I started speaking, she would go hard into prayer before I barely shared the day's issue. Or, if I started crying, she would bust out singing,

"If you want the joy, you must ask for it. If you want the joy, you must ask for it. If you want the joy, you must ask for it. The joy of the Lord is my strength." It was loud and totally random. *Then, she would burst out in laughter*– you get the picture. Soon, we both burst out laughing. I was reminded that having joy in the Sunken Place was a choice that only I could make. I would feel better and empowered to stay in the fight for my husband and our marriage.

My selection of people I considered safe was so small. Small only because I didn't want anyone to think poorly of my husband. I didn't want him judged. However, I understood that I needed some type of coaching from an older, more seasoned wife.

I kept trying to wrap my head around what was happening. I needed some physical assurance that this, too, would pass from someone who had been in my wifely shoes. My friend, Marie Marie, was that person for me.

Man, I never missed my Dad so much during this marriage chapter. He had been gone almost twenty years, and yet in this valley, there were days I cried until I had nothing left because I missed him so much. I desperately needed a man's perspective. I wanted a man that Greg loved and respected to talk some sense into him, basically telling him to get his act together!

My Underdog, the husband of Marie Marie, was that person for me. I called him for clarity around the best way to approach my husband or for a man's point of view. I cried many tears while confiding in the two of them.

The Sunken Place is a very lonely place to be. Although you and your spouse are there together, you are not together. As a wife coach and a teacher for married couples, I would never, ever have encouraged a wife to share her marital struggles with someone who isn't married. Why? Because marriage is so delicate and intricately designed, it really does require a different type of mindset.

However, this is the interesting thing about Grace; it only requires you to be led by the Holy Spirit. It isn't based on best practices or a list of dos and don'ts. It allows Daddy to do what He needs to do, to get you to where He needs you. And the route He

chooses may or may not be one you would have chosen for yourself.

Chapter 18: Speak Life

As my sister and I would share, the Holy Spirit would remind me how very important my choice of words was to my situation. I could be a foolish woman, further tearing down my marriage with my words, or I could be a wise woman building up, encouraging, and strengthening my spouse, my marriage, and myself with my words.

The word says, *we also believe and therefore speak,* (2 Cor. 4:13 NIV). What do you believe about your Sunken Place? In your heart of hearts, what do you believe? The Word also says, "Out of the abundance of the heart his mouth speaks," (Luke 6:45 ESV). At this moment, do you believe you are victorious despite how you feel, what your spouse said, how dire your Sunken Place looks, how long you've been there, someone else's experience, what you googled that wasn't Word?

All day long we're talking. Why not talk about the things that matter and line up with the Word. As a matter of fact, the Word promises that *His Word does not come back void (without producing any effect, useless) to Him, but shall accomplish what I please and purpose and it shall prosper for the thing in which I sent it (Isaiah 55:11 AMPC).*

In the words of Toby Mac, "Speak life."

Chapter 19: Choose & Practice Forgiveness Daily

Once, I read a book that focused on our ability and freedom as people to make daily choices. It reminded its readers that we make choices every day, whether we're conscious of it or not. We choose what time to go to bed, what time to wake up, what we'll wear, what toothbrush we'd like to use, or if we'll take a bath or a shower or not. What we'll eat for breakfast, which way we'll go to work or not. Even if we don't make a choice, it's still our choice to make. You get me?

And then one morning, Joseph Prince shared a scripture in a different version than what I was used to using, and this scripture encouraged believers to adopt a forgive-quickly attitude.

"Be even tempered, content with second place, quick to forgive an offense. Forgive as quickly and completely as the Master forgave you," (Col 3:13-14 MSG).

I also remember a conversation my husband and I had outside of the Sunken Place. We were discussing forgiveness. I'm an easy forgiver, my husband, not so much. During our conversation, I said to him, "But you forgive me."

Greg's response was, "I'm married to you, and I love you, so I have to choose daily to forgive you. If I didn't, we couldn't stay married.

Forgiveness is an act of Love

Grace encourages us to forgive, not in order to be forgiven; that's Law. *We forgive as we have been forgiven-(Ephesians 4:32 NIV)*. This forgiveness was purchased for us at the cross, all our sins, past, present, and future. What I'm simply trying to say, not so simply, is life is full of choices. Sometimes the choices are easy to make. When your spouse is in a place where he or she is consistently making bad decisions that hurt you, your marriage, your finances, your family, or even himself, sometimes the choices are beyond difficult to make. Forgiveness under these circumstances is a hard choice—however, a necessary one for the sake of your marriage. So*, follow the way of love- (1 Cor. 14:1a NIV)* and practice forgiving often and quickly.

Chapter 20: Create Boundaries, Not Ultimatums

T here was no shortage of opportunities provided for me to give ultimatums in the Sunken Place. However, experience has shown me that very rarely do they work. Rarely is the person issuing the ultimatum prepared for the aftermath if the person doesn't make the choice they'd like.

Boundaries create a space for more options which made me feel a little more in control. Creating boundaries isn't usually difficult when you're in a good place. However, when you're in the Sunken Place, it can feel like disciplining a teenager–for a while, you see straight rebellion and then acceptance.

Some established boundaries in the Sunken Place might be: Curfews-there is an old saying, "Ain't nothing open at two in the morning, except legs and liquor stores." Today, we know that there are a lot of places open at and after 2 a.m., none of where a married Christian person should be without their spouse's knowledge or consent. Even if they struggle to keep the curfew, it's important to set a standard of expectations.

Finances

Couples should agree on limiting how much they can or cannot spend without their spouse's knowledge and consent. Have full disclosure of your personal financial status, both individually and collectively.

Family Time

Spending time with family is a must. There will definitely be occasions when time with the family reminds them of the life they're trying to escape. However, family time will also remind them that people love and care about them, want them around, and that they matter. Your spouse needs to know they're important and needed.

Digital Boundaries

It can be hard to know where the line between healthy and unhealthy is once a relationship goes online. What are the rules for Facebook, Instagram, Twitter, Tumblr, Snapchat? What should your digital relationship look like? Before you talk to your partner about your online relationship, check-in with yourself to see what makes you feel comfortable. Whatever rules are set will also apply to you. Start by considering your digital boundaries:

- Is it okay to tag or check in with the opposite sex?

- Do we post our relationship status?

- Is it okay to friend or follow your spouse's friends?

- When is it okay to text me and what the expectation for when to respond to the text?

- Is it okay to use each other's electronic devices?

- Is it okay to post, tweet, or comment about our relationship?

Once you know how you feel, you can talk to your partner and create a digital dating agreement between the two of you. Together, you can decide what feels healthy and what doesn't.

Settingboundaries: loveisrespect.org (reference)

This is less about control and more about respect for one another and the sanctity of marriage.

Chapter 21: Fear Not

There is no fear in love; but perfect love casts out fear~ 1 John 4:18 (NKJV)

Navigating through the unknown was scary. Discovering my spouse was emotionally involved with another woman was ABSOLUTELY FRIGHTENING! Sistah Gurl was officially released, and with her came the spirit of fear. Now, every day fear crept around the edges of my mind threatening to push me in the direction of no return. It took everything in me to not allow my actions to be motivated by fear.

While the un-apology was taking place, I struggled with the pride of letting go of my deep desire to hear him apologize. I struggled with forgiving him. I struggled with trusting Daddy God; simply because I was afraid. Somewhere in the deepest parts of my soul, I was afraid that if I forgave him, if I moved forward without a verbal apology, if I trusted Daddy God with my heart where my husband was concerned, perhaps He wouldn't deliver. I mean, after all, He allowed us to go through this desert experience in the first place. If I let go, would my spouse think that he had gotten away with something, that it was okay to go rogue or hurt me whenever he felt like it without punishment?

When fear would paralyze me, this simple phrase would revitalize me:

Fear is expecting something bad to happen. Biblical Hope is to have a confident expectation of good. I can expect good and not evil! Why? because Jesus loves me! -Joseph Prince

When I gave fear access, I was expecting something bad to happen. So, I made the decision to remember how much Daddy God loves me, loves my husband, and loves our marriage. The more I focused on His love for us, the less I feared. Therefore, 1 John 4:18 became very real to me.

Our trials are temporary, designed to produce character and develop perseverance. The Word calls them the "*testing of our faith"* in James 1:3. So, although I was afraid, I focused on one day at a time to trust Daddy God, not my husband. "He who promised is faithful" (Hebrews 10:23b).

There are tools that were offered and that I had heard others used. However, I would warn against using worldly tools in a spiritual fight.

For we wrestle not against flesh and blood but against principalities, against powers, against the rulers of darkness of this world, against spiritual wickedness in high places

(Eph 6:12 KJV)

Avoid the Iyanla Method

Iyanla Save My Life has a huge following, one mostly comprised of women. She teaches families how to deal with their past hurts in order to fix their future. She has several favorite sayings, "You can't fix what you won't face," and "You need to do your work." These and her other phrases may have some truth and be useful in some situations; however, they are not biblical tools and should not be used in the fight to save your marriage.

All Iyanla tools are but worldly tools designed to fight worldly issues. Your spouse transforming into a seemingly different person overnight is not worldly; it's spiritual. Using the world's tools to fight this spiritual battle causes you to focus on bringing about the needed change. You as the solution, you do the work, you, you, and more you. Because your focus is off God, it becomes, "Look at all that I'm doing right," or "Look at all I am doing to save the marriage. My spouse isn't 'doing the work.' They won't face it, so they can't fix it."

In the previous paragraph, how many times do you see the word "you?" Now, how many times do you see the Lord, God, or Jesus mentioned anywhere in the prior paragraph? That paragraph is what our marriages begin to look like when we apply Iyanla's tools to a Daddy God situation. Your marriage wasn't blessed and anointed by Iyanla or your ancestors. You stood before the Lord God Almighty and pledged your love for your spouse and dedicated your marriage to Daddy God.

Here's an example of what that looks like: "I'm doing everything. My spouse isn't doing anything. He's getting worse. He won't 'do his work.' He can't fix what he won't face." This had been my way of thinking. I became more discouraged about my situation because I had based the success of my marriage on myself and/ or my spouse. However, my spouse is obviously not in a space to ensure the success of our marriage. He/she probably doesn't even understand what they're going through or experiencing. I can't tell you how many times my husband would say something harsh to me and then, in the very next breath, say, "I don't know what's going on with me." Your spouse could possibly be in the midst of a nervous breakdown.

The Word of God encourages us in that, "Those who are strong and able in the faith need to step in and lend a hand to those who falter, and not just do what is most convenient for us" (Romans 15:1 MSG). If currently, you are the stronger spouse, spiritually mature, Daddy God has equipped you to stand in the gap for your spouse, for your marriage to win. Using the tools, he has given you, trust that those tools are all you need!

Chapter 22: Take Care of Yourself

I'm the person that walks around saying, "I'm too blessed to be stressed," AND I really believe it. One day during this chapter of my life, I had a knot in my shoulder, and nothing I did would make it go away. I went to see my doctor. The first thing she asked me was, "What is going on at home?" Then she gave me a referral for a stress test. I was floored! This knot is STRESS RELATED? My husband was trying to kill me!

All I know is STRESS KILLS! Right there, at that moment, I knew I had to get back on my square. I sat in my car that afternoon and had a heart-to-heart with Daddy. I made the deliberate decision to "cast my cares." I put on some worship music and sang all the way home. That night, I built a beautiful affirmation/scripture heart made of post-it notes on my dresser mirror. Every morning when I awoke, I would see my face framed by all the beautiful truths in my life. And I would say them aloud each morning: "I'm beautiful," "I'm fun to be around," "I'm a prize," "Jesus Loves Me," "I am more than a conqueror," "I'm enough," and "I can do all things through Christ that strengthens me," I

WON– you get the gist? My knot went away. The best decision I ever made was to "cast my cares on Daddy God because He cares for me." This was just one good decision among many.

In the Sunken Place, your spouse may lose interest in you, your marriage, your friends, and your family. I went four years without a compliment from my husband. When we went out with friends, he would have something nice to say about each wife. Yet, he would overlook me like I was nothing. This man spent twenty-two years treating me like a queen and intentionally made me feel loved, desired, and wanted by him. I never lacked his attention. Then, suddenly, I was the person he despised being around. Choices, choices, choices! In my hurt, my flesh encouraged me to make all the wrong choices. I struggled daily with thoughts of spending time with other men who found me desirable. I yearned to be held, touched with gentleness, and told I was beautiful. I craved attention.

Funny thing, Daddy God has a way of keeping you when you can't keep yourself. During this difficult period, while my husband found his contentment in the streets, reliving his youth. I often wanted to 1. Also, run the streets to massage my hurt ego 2. Show him I didn't care and 3. Show him he wasn't the only grown-up in this relationship.

My frustration lay in the fact that in the evening when I could have made the worse decisions, my daughter needed my dang car! I was trapped. My husband could get off work or spend 14 to 16 hours a day running the street between work and foolishness. I had to be home by 8:30 p.m. Monday through Friday. Most nights I was livid, obsessed with scrolling Facebook for a sighting of him. At one point, I found myself doing what I encouraged other wives not to do. I became a junior private investigator–ear hustling on his conversations on the rare times he was home, going through his phone, his emails, anything to give me a clue of what I was up against. No wonder I had a stress knot!

I had to put these types of behaviors to rest early on in our marriage for the sake of my mental well-being. I'm a Word baby, "Keep your mind stayed on me and I will give you perfect peace" (Isaiah 26:3 NKJV). My mind was nowhere near at peace. I had allowed this trip to the Sunken Place to knock me off my square; caused me to forget the tools Daddy had given me through His word to keep me at peace.

When I researched midlife crisis, the results were devastating. Spouses spent an overwhelming amount of time and energy focused on the state of their "spouse." And in doing so, let themselves go. I chose to get myself together, not for my husband, but for me. It was the best thing I could do for myself.

Chapter 23: Mentally

Years ago, early in my marriage and recommitment to Christ, I put my alter ego, Sista Gurl, to death. Sista Gurl was who I was during my backsliding years. She was cute, witty, and smart with quick comebacks, or so I thought. My husband saw her as sarcastic, rude, arrogant, mean-spirited, patronizing, and disrespectful.

I was proud of the lengths I went through to kill her, to put her to death. She used her tongue to wreck my marriage, little by little. She didn't know what a "soft hit" was and "only hit below the belt." Every other phrase or comment that came out of her mouth let my husband know that I didn't need him, or that I disregarded him, or I thought I was smarter than him. Her words were meant to cut quick and deep–all Jugular vein action.

After many successful years of keeping her dead and buried with the help of the Holy Spirit, an incident took place while in the Sunken Place where my husband's actions violently awoke her. She came bursting back into my psyche. It felt as though she had kicked a door in with every intention of renewing our relationship. This intrusion back into my life suddenly put me back in the place of feeling insecure and threatened, afraid, defensive, hurt, and desperately wanting to hurt back. With her came the spirit of Inspector Gadget, and suddenly, I resorted back to doing things I had done in our first few years of marriage. It was driving me insane.

I had to find a way to get back on my square and quickly. I realized that the blow that life had just dealt me in my marriage had knocked my focus off. I felt like I was doing a balancing act on a tightrope and couldn't remember where to focus to make it across safely.

The Word tells us that *he will give us perfect peace if we keep our mind stayed on him (Isaiah 26:3 NKJV)*. It also reminds us that if we *meditate on his word day and night then we shall prosper and have much success -(Joshua 1:8 KJV)*. It also reminds us in the Word that *faith comes by hearing -(Romans 10:17 NKJV)*. I needed to hear and then hear some more, and then hear some more, and then hear some more until I was confident of Daddy's love for me. I needed Him to remind me of His ability to keep me, and that this was a very short chapter in a very long book of my life, and this too shall pass. All things, all things, not some, not if you, but *"ALL things work together for my good" (Romans 8:1 KJV)*. And I may not see it right away, I may not see it two years from now, but I will see it! Not on my timing, but on Daddy's timing because He knows best!

Chapter 24: Socially

Instead of recklessly running the streets as I was encouraged to do by Sista Gurl...I chose instead to get out more and broaden my horizons.

In the Sunken Place, our marital friendship was ignored, neglected, and dismissed. I found myself floundering, trying to catch my bearing. I recognized that to make my husband or our relationship my focus was dangerous. I couldn't fix him. The only person I could control was Sarita, and it seemed most important to allow Daddy to keep me while my husband was going through.

I'm really an extrovert, however I would oftentimes get invited to different events. I would accept the invitation and then on the day of the event usually not go. Sometimes it was me. Sometimes it was based on how my husband felt.

In an effort, to broaden my horizons, I began to accept and attend those events. I joined Mastermind groups, a modeling troupe, volunteered for various events, and attended some networking nights. I met wonderful people, gained great new friendships, and had incredible experiences. These things help me not to focus on the rabbit hole my marriage was going down

Physically

I joined my work Wellness Place program; I joined a boot camp and a water aerobics class. I even invited Greg to join me in a boot camp. We had an amazing time getting up together at 4 a.m. to go workout together. Pretty cool. I started walking regularly and changing my diet. I embraced my natural hair and began wearing locs. That was a scary decision because my husband already wasn't feeling me, and I knew that he absolutely loves long, straight hair. And yet, I messed around and got locs. I wasn't sure how that was going to play out. However, being bothered with my hair had become another stressor. So, it was either my hair or my husband something had to go!

Chapter 25: Permission to Grieve

Often when I would think of grief, I would immediately think of death. Over the years I've come to understand that grief is not associated with just death but loss.

I've grieved several losses over my lifetime. When my oldest child came home from her first year of college expecting her first child, I grieved the death of the dream I had for her. With the loss of each house, we tried to buy over the course of twenty plus years, I grieved. When I lost my iPhone with over 1000 contacts, I probably went through all five stages of grief; the struggle was real.

In the Sunken Place, I grieved the loss of our marriage as I knew it. The familiarity, the comfort, the knowing what to expect, the knowing how to respond. What I knew and loved was gone. I had never been in this place before– that of being married and yet alone. I had never not been respected and honored by my husband. I didn't know what it was to not have my thoughts and opinions valued and considered by him.

This was a sadness I had to shake daily. I had to give myself permission and space to process this loss, to consider what my new normal would look like, and then, remind myself that *weeping endures for a night, but joy comes in the morning (Psalm 30:5b KJV).*

Wait for It!

Tell your heart to beat again
Close your eyes and breathe in
Let the shadows fall away
Step into the light of grace
Yesterday's a closing door
You don't live there anymore
Say goodbye to where you been
And tell your heart to beat again

  Tell Your Heart to Beat Again by Danny Gokey

Chapter 26: The Un-Apology

One of my favorite authors, Gary Chapman, best known for the 5 Love Languages, wrote another book called the 5 Apology Languages. Few times in life have I discovered a book so appropriate for this season of my life. Much like the 5 Love Languages, the way you apologize is how you would like people to apologize to you.

The book lists the various forms of apology:

Expressing Regret-Saying, "I'm sorry"

Accepting Responsibility- "I'm sorry. I know I hurt you, and I'll at least try to never do it again."

Making restitution- Making the person feel secure in your love for them

Genuinely repenting- Change of behavior

Requesting forgiveness- "Please forgive me."

For at least five years, our marriage went through hell. It's a period in life I hope to never revisit. When trust has been broken, it is difficult to restore. Most times, even though a person apologizes, no matter how many times they apologize, if the behavior doesn't change, the apology isn't considered sincere, and it's quickly dismissed as such.

As we began to heal, I desperately wanted all five apology languages.

I wanted to hear him say, "I'm sorry. I didn't mean to hurt you. I'll never do it again, please forgive me." In the depths of my soul, it's what I wanted. It's what my flesh wanted.

What do you do when you don't ever hear those words spoken?

During this season of our marriage lies ran rampant. He could have spoken those words, "I'm sorry," a thousand times and I would not have believed him.

"I can show you better than I can tell you," Gregory Sashington

This is one of his favorite statements. Although, I never heard the words, I'm sorry, he began to show me with his actions all the things he couldn't put into words.

He showed me by coming home when he said he would.

He showed by responding to my text.

He showed me by sharing his whereabouts with me.

He showed me by including me in events he was invited to attend.

He showed me by cutting ties with inappropriate friendships.

He showed me by listening, by complimenting me, by spending time with me, and more importantly, by choosing us.

Love is an action word. He went above and beyond to reassure me of his love for me.

This did far more than simply hearing the words, I'm sorry. This was *Genuine Repentance.*

Chapter 27: Hope

A Confident Expectation of Good

Fear is expecting something bad to happen. Biblical Hope is to have a confident expectation of good. I can expect good and not evil! Why? because Jesus loves me! -Joseph Prince

This was the longest and hardest chapter of our marriage together book. It lasted just about seven years. During this season, I reminded myself often of how much Daddy God loves me. I also reminded myself of His promises towards me. I would thank God in advance for the testimony that was going to come from this season. I knew He was working ALL things together for our good and I spoke of it often.

As I write this chapter, Daddy God in His faithfulness, has healed, restored, and delivered us. He has made good on every promise to me regarding our marriage and it just keeps getting better. My husband and I are loving on each other. I am so glad Daddy is who He is.

To say the least, there is still some residue from our journey to the Sunken Place. Sista Gurl still peeks her head out from time to time, usually with quiet carefully placed suspicions or thoughts–thoughts like, "He's been gone all day. Where is he? Who is he with? Is he really where he said he is? Are we really good? Is he really satisfied with his choice to stay? Make no mistakes the thoughts do come.

In the last few years, while Daddy was putting us back together, occasionally I would forget who I am and react from a place of fear. Most times I remember who I am (the Righteousness of God through Christ Jesus). I am His baby girl, and He has provided me with tools. So, instead of reacting negatively, I turn my thoughts to Philippians 4–the peace passage, and I choose to think on those things that are pure, just, noble, praiseworthy, and of good report. The Word says to think on those things and the God of peace would be with me. None of the things that Sista Gurl ever suggested would bring me peace. I'm so grateful for the Word of God.

Today, we're in the space of re-learning one another. For the longest time, all I wanted was for our marriage to go back to the way it was. I wanted my husband to be the man I remembered. I wanted our marriage back. He is never going to be the same man; we will never have the same marriage. How could he be? How could we be the same? We've been through war. If there is one thing I've learned, it is that war changes you. You may get wounded. There will be scars; for me, those scars are a reminder that Jesus is a healer. He makes all things new.

I'm not the same wife I was seven years ago. I'm a better wife, a stronger wife, a more appreciative wife. Greg is not the same husband. He's a better husband, a more attentive husband, a more devoted husband. Our marriage will never be the same! It is a better marriage, a stronger marriage, a marriage with a testimony!

Way Maker,

Miracle Worker,

Promise Keeper,

Light in the darkness

My God, that is who you are, that is who you are

Way Maker by Leeland

To God be the Glory for the things HE has done!

Addendum

Love Letter to Daddy's Favorite Spouse (Offended)

Pray for your spouse! Pray for your situation, for your children, for everything! There is nothing too small. He cares about what you care about! Remember to look for and celebrate the smallest victories. Thank God for His ability to keep, transform, renew, restore, and thank Him for what He's already done!

While you're waiting, take it slow and steady, one day at a time. Stay focused! Right now, you're in the winter season of your marriage. Don't panic, the weather is about to break! Your spring, your time of refreshing and renewal is coming! *Your most painful season is usually where you have the most opportunity for growth.* Daddy God would use this season to teach you how to REST, even in difficult situations.

Ask yourself: *Is there anything too hard for God? (Jeremiah 32:27 KJV). If God is for us who can be against us (Romans 8:31 KJV)? Greater is He that is in you than He that is in the world (1 John 4:4 KJV).*

Remember Daddy *God is no respecter of person (Romans 2:11 KJV)* If He did it for us, He will do it for you! Spend time practicing His presence daily; Read the word. And hear the word daily. "Faith comes by hearing, and hearing (and hearing and hearing) by the Word of God" *(Romans 10:17 KJV). (The extra "and hearing and hearing" was added by me)*

It's not personal. The biggest fight you have is to resist the urge to take matters into your own hands. The only fight you have is to REST. He gave you His only Son, why would He not freely give you ALL things, including your marriage. Daddy God loves you and He is in control!

Love you 🖤 Sarita

#youreanovercomer

#stayinHISpresence

Addendum

Love Letter to Daddy's Favorite Spouse (Offender)

Daddy God loves you! He has not turned His back on you, He has not forgotten about you. You may be angry at Him. He's okay with that, He can handle it. This might be one of the most frustrating times of your life. He still loves you. *He knows the plans He has for you (Jer. 29:11 NIV).*

I encourage you today to receive His grace towards you. The Word says, "*He who receives the abundance of grace and the gift of righteousness shall reign in life through Jesus Christ*" (Rom 5:17KJV). I encourage you to see yourself the way He sees you. *God made him who had no sin (Jesus Christ) to be sin for us, so that in Him we (you) might become the righteousness of God (2 Cor. 5:21 NIV).* Righteousness isn't something you do. As a believer, it is what He gifted you. It's how He sees you. Not your sin, not your situation. He only sees the blood of Christ on you. I repeated this on my worse days, with tears running down my face. I reminded myself of who I am in Him.

It seems too good to be true. Like there's more you need to do. There isn't. Jesus did it all for you at the cross. Be led by Him and watch this situation work out for the good of your marriage.

Jesus Loves you and so do I.

Love you 🖤 Sarita

#youreanovercomer

#stayinHISpresence

Addendum

Daddy God never fails. Once you agree to become a part of His family, all the promises throughout this book are yours. I invite you to receive these wonderous gifts by praying the prayer below.

Prayer of Salvation

Salvation is a gift from God and comes through believing in Jesus and Jesus alone. In John 14:6, the Bible tells us very clearly that Christ is the only way to God and eternal life, and in Romans 10:9-11, the Bible tells us how to be saved and have eternal life: Believe in our hearts that Jesus died for our sins and was raised from the grave and confess with our mouths that Jesus is our Lord and Savior.

To accept Jesus Christ into your life today and be saved, please say this prayer:

"Heavenly Father, thank you for your love for me, for sending Jesus Christ to die on the cross for all my sins. His precious blood washes me clean. You raised Him from the dead. He's alive today. And I thank you that all of my sins are forgiven. I'm righteous by the blood. I'm under God's favor. And I thank you Father that surely goodness and mercy will follow me all the days of my life from this day forth. In Jesus' name. Amen."

Joseph Prince Ministries

Scripture References:

Matthew 7:24-27

2 Corinthians 4:13 NIV

Colossians 3:13-14 MSG

Philippians 4:4-8 NIV

Psalm 27 KJV

1 John 4:18 KJV

Resources:

Destined to Reign by Joseph Prince

K-Love Christian Radio Station

The Power of Prayer to Change Your Marriage by Stormie Omartian

Daddy's Favorite Ministry on Facebook & Instagram

Avoiding the Sunken Place Playlist

Strong Enough by Matthew West

Just Be Held by Casting Crown

Trust in You by Lauren Daigle

My Story by Big Daddy Weave

How He Loves by David Crowder Band

Eye of the Storm by Ryan Stevenson

Tell Your Heart to Beat Again by Danny Gokey

Cast My Cares by Finding Favor

Way Maker by Pentecostals of Alexandria

Grace Wins by Matthew West

Overcomer by Mandisa

Good Good Father by Chris Tomlin

Good Morning by Mandisa, TobyMac

Love Him Like I Do by Detrick Haddon, Ruben Stoddard, Mary Mary

Speak Life by TobyMac

Intentional by Travis Greene

Do It Again by Elevation Worship

Websites

www.JosephPrince.org

http://www.midlifewivesclub.com This is a Christian-based site about midlife crisis and offers a live chat several times a week. This is a support group for people who do not want divorces—and often they do not believe in divorce.

Books:

Men in Midlife Crisis by Jim Conway

How to Survive Your Husband's Midlife Crisis by Gay Courter
& Pat Gaudette

About the Author

Sarita Sashington has three passions in life; Transforming relationships through Grace - which she does weekly through Daddy's Favorite Ministry on Facebook, Marriage, and Parenting. She has a B.A. in Business Management and is the Married Couples Sunday School Teacher at her church.

She enjoys spending time with her family, traveling, reading, and line dancing.

Currently, she resides in Matteson, IL., with her husband of 28 years, her three wildly successful young adult children, and her three beautiful, intelligent, and funny Misha babies!

www.ingramcontent.com/pod-product-compliance
Lightning Source LLC
LaVergne TN
LVHW011335080426
835513LV00006B/364